A Kind of Vesu

A play

Gillian Plowman

Samuel French—London
New York-Toronto-Hollywood

A KIND OF VESUVIUS

First performed by The Flat Four Players with the following cast:

David   Ian Armstrong
Derek   Robert Iles
Ian   David Flint/Christopher Bartle

CHARACTERS

David, a redundant production manager
Derek, a redundant computer programmer
Ian, a redundant sales clerk

The action takes place in an empty room

Time——the present

Other plays by Gillian Plowman
published by Samuel French Ltd

Cecily
David's Birthday
The Janna Years
Me and My Friend
Tippers
Two Summers

A KIND OF VESUVIUS

It is fairly dark. There is no furniture. David is in the room, crouched, listening to haunting music. The music is controlled by David's CD remote control

Derek enters

Derek David? Are you in here?
David No.

Derek switches the light on

Derek You are.
David No. My body is. My soul is elsewhere.
Derek Birmingham?
David What?
Derek Is it in Birmingham?
David No. (*He switches off the music*) Sylvia and the kids are in Birmingham. I said, "Go to Florence. Look at the great paintings of Botticelli, Raphael, Leonardo da Vinci ... Michelangelo's sculptures in the Medici Chapel ... his David which looms so large it almost overpowers the Palazzo behind it ... cross the Ponte Vecchio and see and feel ... the burnt ochre of Florence." They went to Birmingham to see her Auntie Maureen.
Derek Auntie Maureen's all right. She'll spoil the kids rotten.
David She'll diminish them. Rot their teeth, their guts, their souls ...
Derek I was there for ten years and my teeth are all right. So are Sylvia's.
David No books.

Derek She's got books.

David Three on diets and one on dogs. Your Auntie Maureen will buy them videos of an excruciating nature ...

Derek She won't, David. She works in McDonald's. She loves kids. They're kids' videos ...

David Which they watch all night, whilst your Auntie Maureen invites in undesirables, and prattles and drinks and corrupts.

Derek Corrupts what? Who?

David My kids.

Derek She doesn't. She and Donald like having parties and inviting all their friends in and the kids love that. They're allowed to stay up and join in, that's all.

David That's the point.

Derek Yes, well they think so as well. Lots of attention. Sampling a slice of grown-up play time with people who enjoy life. It's bloody miserable for them here.

David So why didn't they go to Florence?

Derek How could they go to Florence?

David On a ferry. On a train. On a coach.

Derek Money.

David I'd have paid for them to go to Florence.

Derek Can I pull the curtains back?

David No. They're nailed together. This is my coffin.

Derek Sylvia said you were depressed.

David Who is Sylvia? What is she?

Derek Your wife.

David I renounce thee, Sylvia. Once, twice, three times I divorce thee. I don't know which way I should be facing. (*He turns around, repeating in each direction*) I divorce thee, I divorce thee, I divorce thee. I divorce thee, I divorce thee, I divorce thee. Which direction should I be saying it?

Derek (*pointing across the stage*) I should do it in that direction.

David Is that Mecca?

Derek No. Birmingham.

David (*in a Birmingham accent*) I renounce thee, Sylvia. Right.

Derek Right.

David Right. That's that done. What can I do for you?

Derek Sylvia said ——

David She's renounced.

Derek Yes ...

David Can't talk about her any more.

Derek My sister said ——

David Who's your sister?

Derek She's the same person as the person we can't talk about any more.

David Her.

Derek Said you were depressed.

David Ha! Ha ha ha! (*He laughs loudly. He sings part of the chorus of "The Sun Has Got His Hat On" while dancing all around Derek. Finally speaking*) I'm Donald. (*He gives a Donald Duck impression and takes an imaginary child by each hand*) Come on, kids, give your Uncle Donald a nice big sloppy whopper. (*He gives the imaginary children a kiss each and passes his hat between the "three" of them*) "The sun has got his hat on" ... Go and get your Auntie Maureen to join in.

Derek (*reluctantly, as Maureen*) No. No, I've got a bone in me leg ... Oh ...

David (*as Donald*) Join in!

They "all" sing the last part of the chorus from "The Sun Has Got His Hat On" while they dance together

David (*as Donald*) And where did Auntie Maureen and I first meet?

All McDonalds!

David (*as Donald*) And what did I ask her for?

All A Big Mac for Donald! (*Pause*) With mayonnaise!

David (*as Donald*) And what has she been getting ever since?

All A Big Mac from Donald! (*Pause*) With mayonnaise, boom boom!

David They're picking up filth when they should be exploring culture.

Derek They don't understand ...

David They bloody do. They bloody understand. "Pass the salad cream, Pol", I said to Polly the other day at tea, and she said,

"Why don't you ask Pete to pass the mayonnaise?" And they both collapsed.

Derek Intelligent children with a sense of humour ...

David Sylvia said, "Your dad and I don't like mayonnaise", and they fell under the table and I told them they were going without supper, and Sylvia said I was a mayonnaise tyrant, and the kids started rolling on the floor in agony and she said now look what I'd done! So ... (*He dances and sings as before. Then he bows*) See. I'm not depressed.

Derek Where's all the furniture?

David That's a stupid question. You passed it in the hall.

Derek It's not easy to get in. It's a small hall.

David It's not out there willy nilly, you know. It's strategically placed to take up the least possible room. I don't want people climbing over it and *complaining* that it's there. Everyone can get past.

Derek Are you decorating? Surprise for Sylvia.

David (*screaming and flapping at Derek*) She who can no longer be named! She who no longer exists! No, I'm not decorating. Decorating?

Derek I could help you.

David That'll be difficult.

Derek Why?

David Because you don't know what I'm doing.

Derek Tell me then.

David Tell me what you're doing?

Derek This minute?

David There is only the present. The past is only the past because now is the present. The future's only the future because now is the present.

Derek Then I'm talking to you.

David What are you gaining from that?

Derek Seriously?

David Yes.

Derek A sense of ... (*He indicates a kind of slipping, of something out of kilter, unbalanced*)

David repeats the gesture. Derek exaggerates it. David repeats that

David A kind of Vesuvius.
Derek Could I get a chair?
David Yes.
Derek Do you want one?
David No.

Derek goes out

David repeats the gesture

Derek returns with a dining-room chair

Derek And one about the Princess of Wales.

David looks at him and comprehends

David She's an amazing woman.
Derek Oh yes. (*He finally places the chair*)
David Increasing your Auntie Maureen's library by twenty-five per cent in one fell biography.

Derek sits in the chair and looks at David. Pause

Wisdom is the only happy human condition, and the best of all civilizations have always searched for it. The Chinese Taoists, the Hindu ascetics, the wise Hebrews, the Islamic Sufis, the Tibetan lamas, the Greek philosophers, the monks of Christianity. They have sought it by denying themselves food and sleep, through chastity, silence, solitude, meditation, and contemplation. I am searching for wisdom, that's what I'm doing. That's why I don't want a chair. That's why I renounce my wife and send my children to Florence. And that's why I no longer subject myself to the rigours of the work place. I exhausted myself with meetings and budgets and profit and loss. Where was the time to reflect? To grow wise.

Pause

Derek I've been made redundant too.

Pause

David You stupid bastard!
Derek Yeah, yeah, I know.
David Just?
Derek A month.

David shakes his head in disbelief

What the fuck do you do?

David puts on Bach's "Toccata and Fugue in D Minor" very loud

David Follow me.

He starts to march about the stage with Derek following him. They march more and more aggressively. The sounds of crowds marching begin to penetrate the music. The cacophony of voices demanding jobs reaches a crescendo and fades

Agitate. Protest.
Derek Yeah, that was good.

They both stand still. Silence. David puts the music on again and they continue the march, with effects as before. They slap each other on the back and walk arm in arm till it all fades and there is silence again. They part

David Unemployment performance. Crowds applauded. Then they all went home.
Derek Yeah.
David So ...

Derek I'm looking ... Anything. But I'm always overqualified for anything.

David Look for wisdom, like me.

Derek Does it pay the mortgage?

David No.

Derek Not a lot of point to it then.

David What about Alan?

Derek Alan?

David Is he being supportive?

Derek I didn't believe it could happen like that. You read about it. Blokes going into work and being told—that's it. No more. Don't come in tomorrow. You'd think, wouldn't you, that they'd have some idea. Did you?

David Some idea, yes.

Derek But I didn't. "Derek, it's the way of the world. We've gone bust. Car keys please. Fortunately you're a single man." (*In a funny voice*) Oh yes, that is fortunate. Very fortunate. Single men do not need food or shelter, least of all self-respect. (*Normal voice*) It's women and children first, last and fucking always, isn't it.

David Something to do with immortality. Looking after women and children. The human race would die out.

Derek You despise me, don't you?

David No! Why? 'Cos you've lost your job? Like me?

Derek No. Because of ... immortality. You've done your bit with your seed. It'll go down the generations, still be going in a million years from now—a little bit of you in the genes. God made people gay so that there wouldn't be any more of them. That's what you think, isn't it?

David No.

Derek Nothing in my genes worth passing on. All those generations before me coming to a grinding halt and not before time, because anything that was worth anything has dwindled to a halt in me! That's what you think, isn't it?

David No. I've never said anything like that. I don't know why you've brought it up.

Derek That's why you've renounced Sylvia. You don't like any of the genes in our family.

David I wouldn't say that. Polly and Pete must have a few and I like them ...

Derek But they're the ones who want to go to Birmingham instead of Florence. You don't like that, David. I haven't told Alan.

David Well I doubt he'd be interested ... oh, that you've been made ...

Derek Redundant! Superfluous! On the scrap heap at thirty-five!

David I thought it was me who was depressed.

Derek You denied it.

David You're supposed to see through that.

Derek Sorry. It's easy to get carried away, isn't it? Get hysterical about life? It's when I think of Alan ...

David He's not a child, Derek. A cherub, maybe ...

Derek Two years it took him to decide to live with me. He's so beautiful. So popular.

David Oh God, Derek ...

Derek He said if I really loved him — you believe that I love him, don't you ...?

David Yes ...

Derek I wouldn't ask him to come to me until I had somewhere special for us to live. So ... I traipsed the streets until I found it ... the house ... I stood outside it and I knew ... you know these things, don't you?

David Doesn't he contribute?

Derek Oh yes. In every way. Alan is everywhere — his pictures, his books, his rugs, and his beautiful, beautiful sculptures ... I mean you talk about Michelangelo, but you should see Alan's. The kids should see Alan's ... they wouldn't have to go to Florence, just Fulham ...

David They're all naked men, and most of them are you!

Derek I am his lover. They're very aesthetic. Michelangelo's *David* is nude.

David But marble. Doesn't he contribute financially?

Derek That's what I do. I come home and there's something new and wonderful every day ... we have a glorious life ... (*He breaks down*)

David You have to tell him.

Derek I can't. Not until I've got something else. (*Pause*) Only I've tried, written, rejects ... nothing.

David I know. You'd think people would want computer programmers.

Derek And production managers.

David Yes. I don't like his sculptures particularly.

Derek There you are, you see. Because they're of me. My genes.

David In a sculpture?

Derek People do like them ——

David I'm a person.

Derek — who understand.

David Derek, he throws lumps of clay together and they're all out of proportion.

Derek Works of art!

David With enormous parts.

Derek That's not true.

David Sell them then. Sell them and pay the mortgage. I wouldn't buy one.

Derek I wouldn't let one anywhere near a soulless bastard like you.

Pause

I've got two months before they repossess.

David It's no relationship, Derek, if you can't be honest with him. You can't protect him from life — it's real, it's insistent, it's cold and bleak and we all have to know that ...

Derek You reckon?

David Tell him. Share it.

Derek No, no, no. I'll think of something. I can't lose him, you see. I can't. I've wanted somebody of my own for so long ...

David He's a parasite. A kept man.

Derek Well, Sylvia's a kept woman.

David When I told her she went to the hospital to increase her hours. "What about the children," they said. "They're bigger now," she replied, "And my husband is at home more." They gave her full-time. She starts next week. She knew what she had to do. She supported me. She's a wonderful woman.

Derek And that's why you hit her.

Pause

David I didn't mean to. I'm not a violent man. You know that, Derek. You know I'm not a violent man. When have I ever done anything to anybody ...?

Derek On Tuesday night to Sylvia.

David She didn't cry out. She didn't shout at me. She never said a word because she knew ... it wasn't me ... I didn't mean to hit her ...

Derek On Wednesday night you hit her ...

David Oh God, oh God ...

Derek On Thursday night she came round and said, "I'm there for him, whatever he needs." And Alan bathed her face with some liniment he makes himself and she came back to you.

David I didn't hit her on Thursday. I didn't. I told her to go to Florence. I told her I was moving the furniture out and searching for wisdom, and that I would never hit her again ...

Derek And I told her to go to Birmingham and stay there.

David She told me she'd be back. She told me she loved me. I don't want that, Derek. Her to go out to work and come home and love me. I don't want it that way round. Oh God, I never meant to do it.

Derek You are disgusting.

David You don't know what it's like. The anger ... and the frustration ...

Derek I know what it's like! But I'd never hit Alan. Never.

David It's different for you.

Derek Why?

David Something goes. Your manhood gets axed by the dole queue.

Derek And hitting a defenceless woman is the only power you have left? That potent, huh?

David You don't understand.

Derek Not long after we went to live with our Auntie Maureen, she had this man for a while — Rubber Trevor we called him because he wore leather underpants, or plastic underpants. Whatever it was, he used to walk around the house in these — and he used to hit Sylvia and me. When Auntie Maureen was doing her shift. Sylvia broke a plate once washing up and he hit her very hard, and I ... I didn't stop him. I was frightened he'd hit me too. So I didn't do anything and he turned on me and asked me what I was staring at and I ran away and he ran after me and he hit me. It happened quite a lot till Maureen found out and sent him on his way. Sylvia could only have been eight and she was always loving me like a little mother. She put her arms round me that first night and we promised each other never to hurt little children or anybody smaller or weaker than ourselves. Only to hit bullies if they were hurting somebody. You're a bully, David.

David I just don't know why ... I can't believe I did ...

Derek She thinks you're depressed enough to kill yourself and I'm supposed to be here to stop you. For her sake, I *am* here to stop you. She's the only woman in the world I love, David. And she loves you. I actually feel like killing you with my bare hands.

Pause

David Death. The ultimate wisdom.

The doorbell rings. They look at each other. Pause

It works on batteries. I don't intend to replace them.

The doorbell rings again. Derek gives David a punch in the guts which floors him

Derek Aren't you going to answer it?
David No.
Derek OK.

Derek goes out

David Goodbye, Derek. Let yourself out. Don't come again. I'm moving into reclusiveness. Hermit-mode. Interior redesign. (*Pause*) Oh Sylvia, your face — your face ...

He puts the music on again — the 1812 Overture. *He feels sick*

> *Derek returns with Ian who carries a bag containing encyclopaedias. Derek switches off the music*

Derek David, this is a Florentine painter. Please get up. This is the householder — a punched man.
David I have to be sick.
Ian Perhaps this isn't a good time .... ?
Derek It's an excellent time. Neither of us have anything to do.
David Except be sick.
Derek That won't take long. Now then, Florentine painter ...
Ian I'm an encyclopaedia salesman. I did tell you.
Derek Yes, you did.
David Oh.
Derek He's disappointed.
Ian I can do you Florentine painters. (*He looks in his encyclopaedia. Reading*) "Florence. Florentia Tuscorum." (*He smiles*) Nice that. "North Italian town, capital of a province of the same name." Florence province — nice that — painters — bridges, piazzas, painters. Ah. "In Florentine painting and goldsmith's work at the time of the Renaissance, the antique was reborn, although it remained much closer to Etruscan forms of experience and art with their constant suggestion of Hellenic influence than to Rome models." Nice that. Suspicious and quarrelsome, it says the Florentines were.
David Not so nice that.
Ian No. Decorating?
David }
Derek } (*together*) No.

Ian looks in his book again

Ian Florin. Now this is interesting. "The original gold florin was first used in Florence in the thirteenth century. It took its name either from the city or from a lily, which was the sign stamped on one of the faces. The florin is known in Germany as a gulden, and the modern Austrian gulden still bears the mark *Fl*. The name "florin" has only recently been introduced into England." (*He smiles at them*) Good that.

Derek Only recently been introduced?

David How old are these books?

Ian "Flotsam."

David Who the hell is this, Derek?

Derek David. You are searching for wisdom. This is an encyclopaedia salesman. (*He spreads out his hands to prove his point*)

David Oh, yes.

Derek What about flotsam? Listen, David, listen.

Ian Listen. Listen. This is fascinating. Jetsam is where goods are cast into the sea, and sink and remain underwater. Flotsam is where they continue swimming on the waves, and Ligan is where they are sunk in the sea, but tied to a buoy in order to be found again.

Derek Sounds like you, me and probably him. Ligan?

David Ligan?

Ian Did you *know* that?

David Yes. No.

Ian Aha!

David Aha yourself, Mr Encyclopaedia Salesman ...

Ian Pettigrew. Ian Pettigrew. At your service, if you want me.

David Do you want him, Derek?

Derek I've a feeling he's out of date.

David Look up Ecu.

Ian Ecu?

David Yes. Go on.

Ian turns the pages

Ian I can do you Ecuador. "A South American republic situated on the equ — ator. (*He pronounces it "Ecu-ator". He laughs at his own joke*)

David No Ecu?

Ian 'Fraid not.

David You're out of date.

Ian Date me. Date me!

Derek What?

Ian Date my encyclopaedias. That's the fun of it. Oh I call at miserable places and everyone ends up having slam jammy.

David Slam jammy?

Ian Fun.

David No they bloody don't. Derek, I'm finding it very difficult to be sick with all this going on. In fact, I've got over it now and I wanted to suffer.

Pause

Ian I'm sorry. I get carried away, I know I do. Excited. The thing is — I'm not after sympathy — people think I am when I start to explain, but I'm not — as they find out if they listen long enough ——

David turns away in exasperation and Ian turns to Derek with his story

I was a clerical officer in the Sales Office of Macey Charles for twenty years. Never had the courage to leave. I wanted to leave and do something different but you know how it is. And then they said ——

Derek Don't come in tomorrow, hand over your car keys.

Ian It wasn't a company car sort of position. I had my own, which I haven't now, of course, but yes, that was the general idea and there I was with no job and I felt so excited.

Derek Excited?

Ian Change of life. Do something different, Ian Pettigrew, I told myself, whilst in the throes of my excitement. Don't do something you don't want to do for the next twenty years. What do you do, may I ask?

Derek Computers. I'm in computers.

David *Was* in computers. He *was* in computers.

Derek I will be again. Flotsam me — continue swimming.

David Surely you're the one who's tied to a buoy?

Derek Ha ha very funny ...

Ian And do you want to be in computers for the next twenty years?

Derek Frankly, yes.

Ian No, you don't. You want to explore other skills, other talents. What are you active in at the moment?

Derek I beg your pardon?

Ian Clubs, societies. What are you currently learning?

Derek That I can't pay the mortgage.

Ian The so-called security of the past can no longer be trusted. Reward for long service can no longer be expected as a matter of course. You have to reformulate your attitudes so that you are ready for anything. Be prepared to stretch yourself, develop your other potentials ...

David Do they still need bouncers at night clubs?

Ian Probably, yes! Be a bouncer!

David Practise that, Derek.

Ian Be willing to consider alternative types of employment ——

Derek and David start to bounce Ian out

— hey! What are you doing? Develop and create new ideas, like car boot sales, or bed and breakfast — I'm trying to help you, you invited me in ...

Ian's voice fades as they exit. David and Derek return to the room

David What about his encyclopaedias?

Derek Out of date. (*He picks one up*) No date.

David No date on this one.

They both pick up another

No. No dates.

Derek Look up computer.

David does so

David Not there. "*Comus* in the later period of Greek mythology
was the god of mirth, revelry and feasting. He was represented as
a drunkard." Sounds like Auntie Maureen's Donald. (*He returns
to the book*) Did Rubber Trevor ever make a pass at you?

Derek No. Nor at Sylvia, if that's what you're thinking. He just hit
us.

David She wouldn't have told me. Never tells me anything that
makes me feel sorry for her. Jesus Christ. And now I've hit her.

Pause

Derek No aeroplanes.

Pause

No cars? Any *motor* cars?

David No motor cars.

Derek Look up Queen Victoria. See if she's dead yet.

David Yes. She died in 1901. Succeeded by Edward the Seventh.
Look up Edward the Seventh.

Derek looks through his book

Derek Picture of the small intestine of the mouse, that's under
"Digestion"; picture of Edinburgh, no cars — that's nice. (*Mim-
icking Ian*) Ah, here they are. All the Edwards — the First, Third
and Fourth were the most noted while the Second, Fifth and Sixth
were each somewhat unfortunate in the circumstances of their
lives ... probably lost their jobs. Or their heads.

David And the Seventh?

Derek Is still alive!

David And he died in 1910. So they were printed sometime
between 1901-1910!

Ian appears

Ian See. I told you you'd be having fun in no time at all.

David How did you get in?

Ian Back door's not locked. You forgot to pay me. You kept the encyclopaedias and you didn't pay me.

Derek We didn't keep them. You forgot them. We don't want the encyclopaedias. Take them.

Ian Twenty-five pounds, please.

Derek What?

David Mr Pettigrew — push off.

Ian produces a gun

Derek He's got a gun, Dave.

David Yes ...

Ian Move over there, next to each other. Right. Nice that.

Pause

David What do you want?

Ian Twenty-five quid for the encyclopaedias.

David You got twenty-five pounds?

Derek No. (*He counts his money*) Seven pounds and something. Got my cheque book.

Ian No, no. No cheque book.

David I sent my cash to Birmingham.

Ian Nobody's ever got any money.

David Sorry.

Ian Sit on the chair then.

David and Derek look at each other. David sits

Both of you.

He makes Derek sit on David's lap

Feel silly now, don't you?

No reply

That's how I feel, every time I knock on someone's door. I was really happy in the office, you know. I'm a shy person. You wouldn't believe that, would you? Not the way I've managed to overcome it. Everybody knew me there. "Morning, Ian," they'd say. (*He waves his gun at them, nodding for them to react*)

David Morning, Ian.

Derek Morning, Ian.

Ian Morning. Stacey's phoned in about their order this morning. (*He waves the gun at them*)

Derek Did they?

David What about the order, Ian?

Ian Five thousand short. Five thousand. How can that be? They signed the delivery note, didn't they?

David Yes.

Derek Yes.

Ian You sure?

David I think they did.

Ian Get me the delivery notes, will you?

David Derek, get the delivery notes.

Derek Where are they?

David Where are they, Ian?

Ian Blue file.

Derek gets up tentatively

Derek Over here?

Ian Yes! Yes! Get them.

Derek picks up the imaginary file

Got them.

Derek Uh ... yes.

Ian Let's see. There you are. Five thousand short. Signed and kept secret. You know what that means, don't you?

David Not quite sure, Ian.

Ian Someone has stolen the other five thousand. (*He glares at them accusingly*)

Derek
David } (*together*) It wasn't me.

Ian I was too good for them, you see. Too honest. "Ian," they said
— first name terms with the bosses — "you got to slip and let slip.
Everybody does it. It's business." And the next day, I was
redundant. Sit down.

Derek sits on David's lap again

Do something else, my wife said. Lydia, my wife. She's sick. I
thought about what I was good at, what I liked doing, what I was
interested in, and it was all just looking after her and going to the
office. Then I saw this advert for an encyclopaedia salesman and
I started, and every time I knocked on someone's door I felt as silly
as you two feel sitting on that chair together. I couldn't do it.

David I think you do it very well.

Ian "It's such a bloody awful world," one man said to me, "Who
the hell wants to know any more about it." I never sold any. "For
your children's future," I said. "What fucking future?" Excuse me
but that's what he said. Not one set.

Derek You get a set for your kids?

David I would do, yes. If you knocked on my door, yes.

Ian I got the sack.

David shouts with pain

What?

David Cramp. he's heavy.

Ian Oh.

Ian drops the arm holding the gun. Derek risks standing

Lydia was proud of me. Losing one job, and picking myself up
and finding another. She can't go out a lot and I had to sell the car,
you see, so I was hoping to save up and buy another one, which
is very difficult if you're not earning any money, and I had this
idea that if people didn't want to bother about today and the future,

what about the past and I looked in the secondhand bookshops and thought about buying old sets of encyclopaedias and selling them, because the past is interesting, and nostalgia and discovering how things were, and there are things in old encyclopaedias that have been left out of new ones, and nobody ever came to see me from the office, never asked how Lydia was getting on, and I thought one day I was going to get a gold watch.

Derek I think that's a good idea. Selling old encyclopaedias. Brilliant idea. You're very good at it.

Ian points the gun again

Ian You didn't buy them.

Derek No, but we would have done ... the way you looked things up and read them out to us, that was good.

Ian I've been practising.

Derek It was good. I think, for people like us who have been made redundant, it's a very good thing to do — read encyclopaedias. Brilliant idea. We just can't afford to buy them. However, perhaps the Social Services *would* buy them in order to issue to the unemployed. Have you thought of that?

Ian You're talking rubbish.

David That's because he's frightened of your gun.

Ian looks at the gun almost with amazement and slowly starts to cry

Ian I love her so much and I've got to be strong.

David That's it, Ian. Always got to be strong. And then what happens when you can't do it?

Ian You know what I thought? If I didn't have her, I mean if she got so ill she died, I wouldn't have to be strong and I wouldn't have to — be a man. When my mother died, all her ambitions for me died with her, and I felt so free. She wanted me to be the mayor. And now I've thought that about Lydia. I'm sorry. I shouldn't be telling you this. You'll despise me.

David No we won't.

Ian Won't you?

Derek David despises me.

Ian Why?

Derek Because I'm gay.

Ian Gay?

Derek Homosexual.

David Not that.

Derek Because I run ragged around a kept spoilt man. I don't treat him as an equal. I treat him as a god. I let him drain me. I'd die if he left me. I'm less than a man.

Ian That's not as bad as wishing your wife dead. Oh my God, just saying it — how can I? How can I say it?

David Thinking — saying's — not as bad as doing. If we're having a competition for unreasonable behaviour, I'm streaks ahead. Aren't I, Derek?

Ian What have you done then?

David I hit my wife. She's got a terrible face now. She's taken it to Birmingham, and she's done that so that I can't look at her and hate myself for what I did. You must both despise me.

Long pause

Derek Should we look something up, do you think?

David Yes. OK.

Ian In the encyclopaedias?

David Yes. Acquire some wisdom.

Ian What?

David Michelangelo's *David*.

Ian looks it up. He still holds the gun but gets excited about the books

Ian Hundreds of Davids.

David Who?

Ian David, Felicien. French composer —— (*He looks at David*)

David (*singing*) "Allons enfants de la patrie ..."

Ian David, Ferdinand. Famous teacher of the violin ... (*He looks at Derek*)

Derek violins a tune

David, Gerhard. A Dutch painter ...

David mimes painting

A very old Dutch painter — 1450-1523 ...

David mimes an old man painting

Nice that. David, Jacques Louis. A painter of the modern French school ...

Derek mimes painting and sings "Allons enfants de la patrie"

David, Saint. Patron saint of Wales ...

David and Derek stand with their hands together in prayer and sing "We'll keep a welcome in the hillside"

David the First. King of Scotland ...
David Och aye the noo.
Ian David the Second. King of Scotland ...
Derek Och aye the noo, two!

Ian laughs

Ian Michelangelo's *David*. "It is David's character which is the dominating element; his is a heroic conception of human will — vigorous, troubled, brave and free. Perhaps for this reason, Michelangelo did not give *David* ideal physical proportions. The head and limbs are too large for the body, thus discouraging admiration of physical beauty as an end in itself."
Derek Michelangelo's *David* is out of proportion! Hah! He said Alan's work was out of proportion and all the time Michelangelo's *David* is out of proportion ...
David For a reason.

Derek And Alan's! Lumps of clay thrown together, you said, with big parts! Michelangelo's *David* has big parts!

David Not the same parts.

Derek What does it matter which parts?

David And not thrown together. Carved out of marble. An incredible, beautiful, expensive, immortal hunk of marble.

Derek He's back to immortality. He despises me because I haven't got any immortality. Have you, Ian?

Ian What?

Derek Passed your genes on?

Ian No. Well, only to the jumble ——

Derek Your genetical genes?

Ian No.

Derek No children?

Ian No ...

Derek Look up genes, Ian. That'll be interesting. We'll look up genes whilst he despises us both.

Ian fumbles for the book one-handed, then absently passes the gun to David. Ian looks in the book

Ian No genes.

Derek Well, there you are. Not yet invented.

David Discovered.

Derek People obviously managed without genes for centuries.

David You can have your gun back, Ian.

Derek Not loaded?

David Not real.

Ian I couldn't afford a real one. You can have the books for seven pounds and something. I know where I can get another set for four pounds fifty. I still make a profit.

Derek All right.

Ian I have got a child. Not Lydia's. She doesn't know about it. She says that men aren't faithful and that she is truly blessed because her husband — me — has never touched another woman in all the time we've been married. Well, it was true to say that I had never touched any woman till Lydia and that was after we were married, and then I wanted to make love to other women as well, once I found out what it was like. And I deliberately went and did it. Told Lydia I was working late, and went to bars and met women. Please let me tell you this. I've never talked to anyone before. Strange. Men talk about football, don't they? Or work?

Derek Or women.

Ian Oh, not so strange then. I'm talking about women. Ha, ha.

David I think you're talking about yourself.

Pause

Ian Yes.

Pause

David Go on, then.

Ian I had a lot of sex with a lot of women and I'm not proud of it but I enjoyed it and when I went back to Lydia, I thought I like you best, Lydia, and I'm an experienced man. It was flattering in a way, wasn't it, for me to like her best? Then a lady called Hester told me she was pregnant and she had *my* baby. And I held it once, and somewhere in this world is Ian Pettigrew's son. And that's all I wanted to say.

David A son not knowing his father?

Derek I didn't know mine.

David And look at you!

Derek There you are, you do despise me ...

Ian Look at me! Look at me. Not much to know. He's better off not knowing me. But he would have been safe with Hester. (*He gets up*) Thank you. Goodbye.

He shakes hands with David

Thank you. Goodbye.

He shakes hands with Derek. Derek gives him the seven pounds and something

Ian goes out

The front door slams

David Do you think she'll come back to me, Derek?

Derek Yes.

David You told her to stay in Birmingham.

Derek She never did anything I said.

David How do you think he managed to have sex with a lot of women?

Derek What do they see in him?

David Yes.

Derek Enthusiasm?

David Enthusiasm. My God! Enthusiasm! Where did it go? Swept under the ashes of time. Lost in the dark ages of the present day. I thought wisdom was a good idea. Enthusiasm is a brilliant concept.

Derek Is it?

David Yes. All those women had sex with Ian Pettigrew because he was enthusiastic. Lydia lies in bed admiring his enthusiasm ...

Derek You don't know that. She could be exhausted by it and that's why she's lying in bed.

David No. That's why she's hanging on to life. We bought his encyclopaedias because he was enthusiastic.

Derek Because he had a gun ——

David And Hester has raised a son with enthusiastic genes in him. That wouldn't have happened without Ian Pettigrew.

Derek Right then. Auntie Maureen's enthusiastic.

David What?

Derek Isn't she?

David What about?

Derek Donald. McDonalds. Your kids. Parties ——

David No she's not.

Derek Yes she is. You can't have one rule for Ian Pettigrew and another for Auntie Maureen. That's discriminatory. Why don't you like her? She thinks you're OK.

David Because she's always over the top.

Derek Over the top is enthusiastic.

David She's an embarrassment. Dancing on tables in pubs, that's what your Auntie Maureen does.

Derek Enthusiasm by any other name! Come on, admit it. (*As Auntie Maureen*) Oh David, my lovely, cuddly nephew-in-law! Come and dance with little Mo!

"She" starts to dance the cancan and grabs David to dance with "her", David gradually accepts the truth of what Derek has said and the cancan gets wilder as the two of them dance and sing

David I'm lucky. My wife's salary will get us by. No more higher rate tax. I can do the house for her. I can do that. I'll culturize the kids. Library books are free. Music cassettes. Can you get CDs in the library? Have to find out. Will I shop? Yes, I'll shop. Museums are free. I'll have conversations with people, not just rapid "How are you? Fines'". In-depth stuff. I'll deal with correspondence. Have time to question the electricity bill, and the telephone bill, and the tax man. They've all been getting away with murder because I haven't had the time, or the energy, Derek. That job's been using up all my energy. It's been using up my life. Derek, I'll make curries. And spaghetti! Using all different spices. They're cheap. Little packets of exciting spices — oregano, turmeric, coriander, asafoetida ——

Derek What?

David You think I know nothing? I'll know a million things. I'll do a million things! What are you going to do, Derek?

Derek Go round the world!

David What about Alan?

Derek Do voluntary service overseas. They pay your fare. I must have something to offer emerging countries. Computers, accounts ——

David Write me letters.

Derek Write you letters.

David And I'll write you letters. Long and interesting and philo-
sophical. They'll publish them when we're dead and someone
will act them in the round at the Manchester Royal Exchange.

Derek I'll let the house.

David What about Alan?

Derek Maybe he'll come with me. Do you think he'd come with
me? He could teach sculpture, couldn't he? He could teach art. He
could show them how to make his liniment.

David He could, yes. I wonder how Sylvia's face is? What if he
doesn't want to go with you?

Derek Then he'll have to pay rent for his room in the house, and be
prepared to share it with at least three other people. There are four
rooms.

David Well done.

Derek I'm sure he'll come with me, though.

David I'm sure she'll come home soon.

Derek Shall we put the furniture back?

David Yes. No! We'll redecorate! This will be a beautiful room for
Sylvia's homecoming. She loves roses. There'll be roses on the
walls. Come on, Derek. Let's decorate!

*He puts more music on: the "Carousel" waltz. There is a light effect
of roses which revolves round the room as David and Derek busy
themselves "painting and papering". David makes a pile of the
encyclopaedias so that he can stand on them to "reach"*

Derek! I'm going to make new curtains. Those ones that do that.
(*He makes loops with his arm*) She'll love me, Derek.

Derek Yes.

*But the lights and sound fade and a deep depression comes over
them both*

David I feel terrible. How does your Auntie Maureen keep it up?

Derek She doesn't always. I've seen her cry.

David Have you?

Derek When she was bathing Sylvia's bruises. She was weeping, really weeping ... she was doing Sylvia's back and Sylvia didn't see, and I knew it wasn't just because of the bruises but because she'd had to send Rubber Trevor away. She loved him, you see. But she loved us. When she saw me looking, she said, "Life's a bugger sometimes, Derek, and it helps to have a little cry."

Pause

David She doesn't need encyclopaedias, does she?
Derek Well, she's not very tall.
David Wisdom. Life's a bugger, Derek, and it helps ...

He begins to cry and turns to Derek and they hug each other

The Lights fade to Black-out

CURTAIN

FURNITURE AND PROPERTY LIST

On stage: CD unit, with CDs
              Curtains at window closed

Off stage: Dining-chair (**Derek**)
              Bag containing encyclopaedias (**Ian**)

Personal: **David**: CD remote control
              Derek: £7 and some small change in pocket
              Ian: gun

LIGHTING PLOT

Property fittings required: nil
Interior. The same scene throughout

To open: Black-out

Cue 1	**Derek** switches on the light *Bring up general interior lighting*	(Page 1)
Cue 2	"Carousel" waltz plays on CD *Revolving rose effect*	(Page 27)
Cue 3	**Derek:** "Yes." *Fade revolving rose effect*	(Page 27)
Cue 4	**David** and **Derek** hug each other *Fade to black-out*	(Page 28)

EFFECTS PLOT

Cue 1   To open   (Page 1)
            Haunting music from CD player

Cue 2   **David** switches off the music   (Page 1)
            Snap off music

Cue 3   **David** puts on music   (Page 6)
            Bach's "Toccata and Fugue in D Minor" plays loudly

Cue 4   They march more and more aggressively   (Page 6)
            *Bring up sounds of crowds marching with voices
               reaching a crescendo; fade all effects*

Cue 5   **David** puts the music on again   (Page 6)
            *Bach's "Toccata and Fugue in D Minor" play loudly
               with crowds marching and voices as before;
               then fade*

Cue 6   **David**: "The ultimate wisdom."   (Page 11)
            Doorbell

Cue 7   **David**: "I don't intend to replace them."   (Page 11)
            Doorbell

Cue 8   **David** puts on music   (Page 12)
            "1812" Overture plays

Cue 9   **Derek** switches off the music   (Page 12)
            Cut music

Cue 10   **Ian** goes out   (Page 25)
            Front door slams

Cue 11   **David** puts on music   (Page 27)
            "Carousel" waltz plays from CD

Cue 12   **Derek**: "Yes."   (Page 27)
            Fade music